EXTREME
BIOLOGY

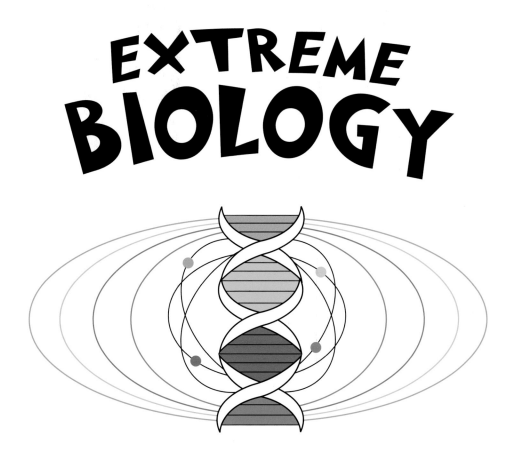

KINGFISHER
NEW YORK

KINGFISHER
LONDON & NEW YORK

Text and Design Copyright © Toucan Books 2013
Based on an original concept by Toucan Books Ltd.
Illustrations copyright Simon Basher 2013

Published in the United States by Kingfisher,
175 Fifth Ave., New York, NY 10010
Kingfisher is an imprint of Macmillan Children's Books, London.
All rights reserved.

Consultant: Francesca Norris

Designed and created by Basher www.basherbooks.com
Text written by Dan Green

Dedicated to Eric and Rufus Ellison
Distributed in the U.S. and Canada by Macmillan, 175 Fifth Ave., New York, NY 10010

Library of Congress Cataloging-in-Publication data has been applied for.

ISBN: 978-0-7534-7051-0

Kingfisher books are available for special promotions and premiums.
For details contact: Special Markets Department, Macmillan,
175 Fifth Ave., New York, NY 10010.

For more information, please visit www.kingfisherbooks.com

Printed in China
9 8 7 6 5 4 3 2 1
1TR/1212/UTD/WKT/140MA

CONTENTS

Introduction
Extreme Biology

The things that live on this planet of ours have the ability to surprise us over and over again. As soon as we think that we have biology nailed, something crops up that blows things apart again. The closer we look at life, the more incredible we discover it to be. Did you know, for example, that you have fewer genes than most grapes do? Or that there are more foreign cells living on your skin and in your intestines than there are cells in your body? Welcome to the extreme side of life!

When it comes to biology, there's always something that needs explaining, and that's what someone like U.S. scientist Craig Venter tries to do. When it comes to the science he adores, Venter is a wild kinda guy who enjoys tearing along at (some might say) unsafe speeds. He loves racing dirt bikes and motorboats—that's when he does his best thinking, he says. Venter is constantly pushing deeper and deeper into the biological jungle, searching for ways to make brand-new life that has never existed in nature. Whatever it is that he brings back, it may some day change the world. This life sure is a riot!

Craig Venter

Chapter 1
Hard-core Herd

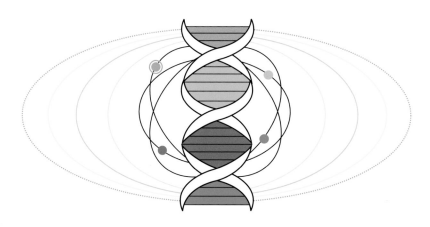

Most living things are fussy about where they live. For example, you feeble humans tend to cluster in Earth's Goldilocks Zone, where it's "not-too-hot" and "not-too-cold." You wouldn't even think about living with crushing pressures, burning radiation, body-popping vacuums, or skin-stripping acid! Not these heavy-duty organisms, though. No, sir—the world holds no fear for this posse of hard-bitten mini heroes! This gritty crew can survive and thrive in the harshest of environments. They'll call almost any place home—some can even live in outer space! Come and meet them . . . if you think you're tough enough!

Tardigrade

Conan the Bacterium

Planarian

Superbug

Tardigrade
◉ Hard-core Herd

✳ Invertebrate animal that survives environmental extremes
✳ Survives by slowing down its body processes
✳ This superdurable dude is also known as a water bear

Don't be fooled by my cute and cuddly nickname, I'm a grizzly old guy. I lumber around on eight stubby legs with clawed feet and look just like a tiny bear. *Grrr!*

Actually, I'm a peaceful soul that loves nosing around in moss and lichen. But I'm built like a tank with my hard outer shell. You can find me in the Himalayan Mountains, in the ocean depths, or living under layers of solid ice! (Soak a bit of moss in water and seek me out with a magnifying glass.) I can cling onto life just one degree above absolute zero. *Brrr!* Put me in a frying pan and I'll grin and *bear* it—up to 300 °F (150 °C). I can survive for 10 years without water. When times are tough, I go into "suspended animation." No worries or strife for me—I curl up, slow down my systems, and wait for better days.

● First described: 1773 (Johann August Ephraim Goeze)
● Size: 0.3–0.5mm (the biggest are 1.5mm) long
● Survival record: 10 days in outer space; 120 years on Earth

Tardigrade

Conan the Bacterium

◉ Hard-core Herd

✳ AKA *Deinococcus radiodurans* and a likely star of the future
✳ A hardy type that can withstand an acute dose of radiation
✳ First Earth traveler on a crewed mission to Mars (sadly failed)

Hard-boiled just doesn't cut it as a tag for me. I hold the Guinness World Record for the toughest bacterium on Earth. I laugh in the face of acid attacks, scorn searing heat, and shrug off numbing cold. To top it off, I love nothing better than a deadly dose of radiation!

Hanging out in cow pies and elephant dung was my thing until I shot to fame in the 1950s. I showed up in trials for sterilizing food with radiation, where I was literally the last man (well, microbe) standing. I can repair radiation-damaged DNA and have been put to work in nuclear plants, gobbling up radioactive waste. My future's bright, too. I can look forward to being tinkered with so that, one day, I may produce medicines in space and store information safe from nuclear disaster. Heroic stuff, huh?

● Discovered: 1956 (Arthur W. Anderson)
● Size: 0.0015–0.0035mm in diameter
● Named after the hard-bitten, 1930s pulp-fiction hero Conan the Barbarian

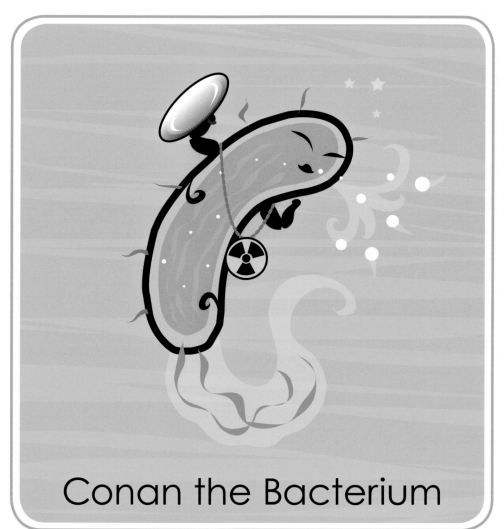

Conan the Bacterium

Planarian

◉ Hard-core Herd

✳ A flatworm that lives in both salt water and fresh water
✳ This wriggler can regenerate any part of its body
✳ Stays forever young by keeping its telomeres nice and long

Immortality is my game! I may not look like a typical hero—all googly eyes and not much brain—but I can *worm* out of any sticky situation. I have regenerative powers that let me regrow body parts. Chop me in two and I'll shrug, chuckle, and make two new worms. Hey, I don't give up that easily!

I have two tricks up my sheath. The first is a stash of "master template" stem cells that can blossom into any type of specialized body cell. The second is an ability to activate an enzyme that keeps my telomeres from wearing out. Telomeres work like the caps on the ends of shoelaces and protect DNA sequences when a cell divides. For many, these caps wear thin with time, which means that genetic information gets lost or damaged, and an organism starts to age. Not for me, though—I'll keep wriggling forever!

● Discovery of telomeres: 1978 (Elizabeth Blackburn)
● Size: 0.3–2.5cm (some giant forms reach 60cm) long
● Other biological "immortals": *Turritopsis nutricula* jellyfish; lobsters

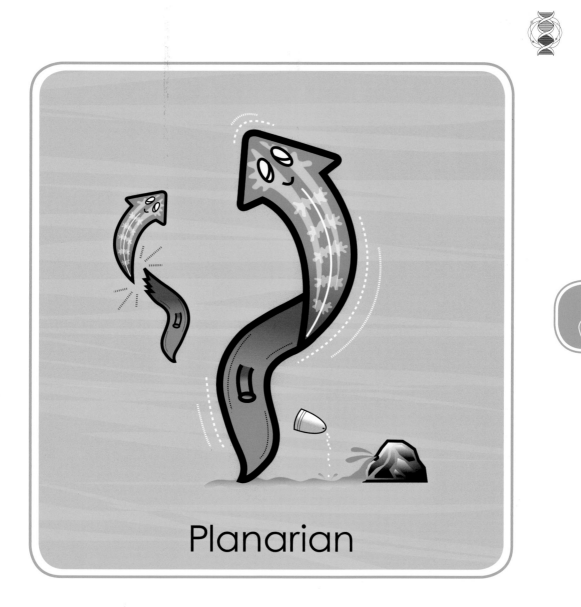

Planarian

Superbug
◉ Hard-core Herd

☀ This dude is a mini mite with maxi malice
☀ A microorganism that's resistant to antibiotic drugs
☀ Examples include hospital bugs *Clostridium difficile* and MRSA

Full of spite and ready to fight, I'm chortling with glee 'cause I'm turning humans' best defenses against them. I have evolved a resistance to drugs that ward off bacterial invasions, and I'm fast becoming invincible!

Antibiotics might be the wonder drugs of modern times, but there's a chink in their armor—when they kill disease-carrying microbes, they also weed out the weak. That means less competition for me, which, coupled with my super-resistance, can be fatal. Worse still, antibiotics can harm colonies of healthy bacteria that keep me and my super-resistance at bay. It's a case of what doesn't kill me makes me stronger! My real enemies are good hygiene, hand washing, and, if you're taking antibiotics, making sure you complete the course.

● Size: 0.0006mm long (MRSA); 0.003mm long (*Clostridium difficile*)
● All the bugs living in and on you: 100 trillion cells
● Number of deaths from multidrug-resistant tuberculosis: about 150,000 per year

Superbug

Chapter 2
Gene Genies

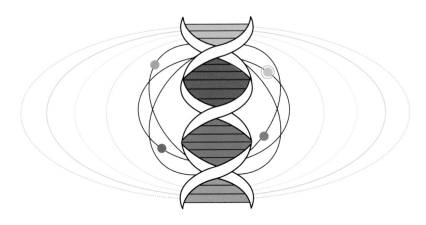

Before meeting the microscopic geniuses who keep life on Earth running, let's look at DNA—the strange stuff that looks like snot and is crammed into nearly every cell of your body. In humans, tiny strands of this DNA are coiled into 23 pairs called chromosomes, which are scrunched into a ball and sit inside a cell's nucleus. When the cell divides to make fresh copies of itself, the DNA unravels to reveal Gene (well, thousands of genes, in fact). Each one is a length of DNA code with instructions for producing certain proteins. And everyone knows that Protein is the stuff of life. You didn't, huh? Hmm, better read on, then!

Gene

Genome

Protein

Gene Expression

Epigenetics

Gene

◉ Gene Genies

✹ Strips of DNA code found in their thousands on chromosomes
✹ Its discovery led to a greater understanding of how life works
✹ All humans have one half set of genes from each parent

Hey, get with the program! Hard-wired on chromosomes and plugged into the core of your body's cells, I am the software that keeps you up and running. I'm just one of the tens of thousands of short stretches of DNA code that instruct a cell to produce lots of different types of Proteins.

I'm locked inside a cell's nucleus, and my instructions need to be copied and transported out of there before they can be run. My pal Gene Expression is itching to tell you all about it. The bottom line is that my instructions are capable of making new copies of themselves. This is the key to passing genetic traits down through the generations, which is how you get to look like your mom and dad. So if you have a complaint about that huge schnoz of yours, perhaps you should take it up with one of them!

● DNA: stands for deoxyribonucleic acid
● Length of DNA inside a cell nucleus: about 7 ft. (2m)
● Only cell without a nucleus: red blood cell

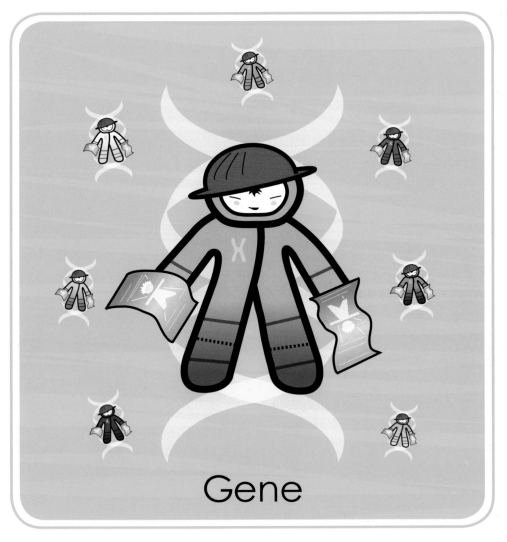

Gene

Genome
◉ Gene Genies

☀ The complete set of an organism's DNA
☀ Two percent of the genome comprises protein-coding genes
☀ Human beings are genetically 99.9% similar to each other

I am a central library, housing all the knowledge needed to completely describe an organism. Contained in my coded depths are all of Gene's programs and subroutines, as well as a raft of noncoding sequences of DNA to boot.

DNA is made of two spiraling strands, chemically linked together by pairs of "bases." Each base joins up with another one to form a rung on DNA's twisty ladder, made up of base pairs arranged in groups of three. The 3.2 billion base pairs in the human genome would fill 5,000 books like this one. Amazingly, the data is almost identical, no matter what living thing you're looking at. But even so, differences are key: eye color, hair color, long second toes—they're all caused by tiny (0.1 percent) changes in genes. A mere two percent difference (15 million base pairs) is what makes you a human and not a chimp. Banana, anyone?

● Term invented: 1920 (Hans Winkler, University of Hamburg, Germany)
● Number of genes contained in a human genome: around 23,000
● Number of base pairs in a human genome: around three billion

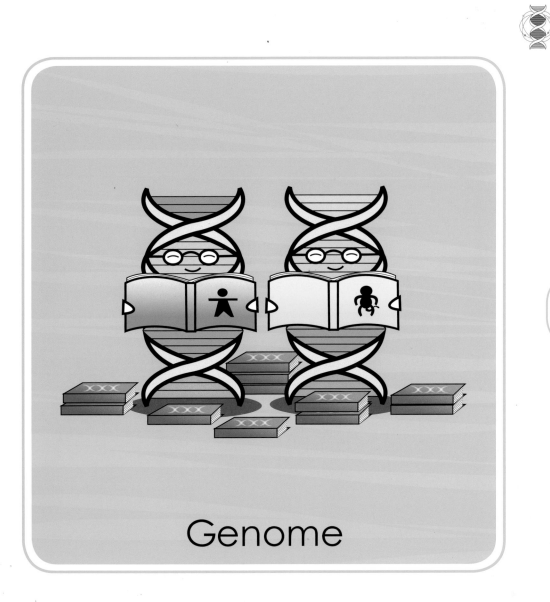

Genome

Protein

Gene Genies

- The stuff that all life is made of
- Carries out all the essential functions in a cell
- Built inside the cell using up to 20 different amino acids

I'm the unsung laborer in this body-building bunch! A solid, no-nonsense type, I buckle up my tool belt and get the job done. I build body tissues—skin, muscle, hair, and nails—I aid digestion, clot blood, break down starch, and control blood-sugar levels. As enzymes, I "catalyze" (see Glossary) chemical reactions inside your body. As hormones, I send chemical messages. You name it, I do it!

You get a lot of me from your diet. These proteins are broken down into amino acids, which are then used (following Gene's instructions) to construct the new proteins your body needs. Fellow worker Gene Expression makes me inside the cell, with the help of a chemical gizmo called a ribosome (also a protein), and then I'm released to do my work in the body. And what work it is!

- Number of different proteins in the body: about five million
- Most abundant protein in the body: collagen (25–33% of body weight)
- Number of ribosomes per cell: approximately 15,000

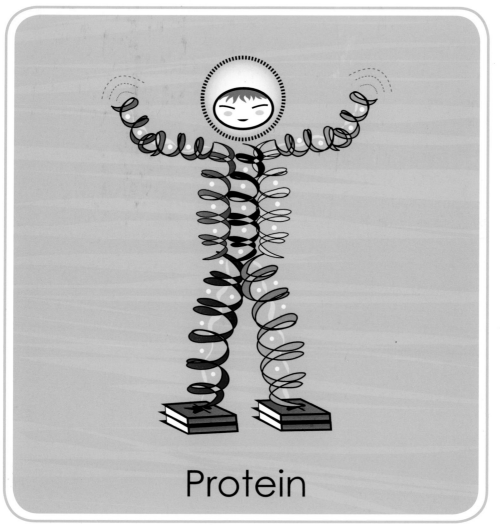

Protein

Gene Expression
◉ Gene Genies

☀ "Reads" genes and translates them into proteins
☀ Proteins are made only in certain parts of the body
☀ Uses a two-stage process: transcription, then translation

Poor Gene can't leave a cell's nucleus, so I need to step in to help. First, I transcribe (copy) DNA strips inside the cell, one base at a time. My new strips leave the nucleus with Gene's instructions on board. Once outside, the strip attracts a ribosome, which begins to build made-to-order proteins (that's the translation stage of my process).

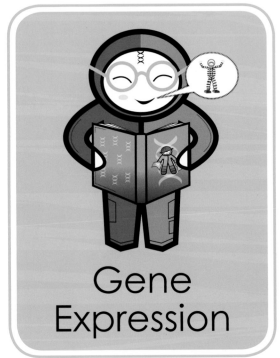

Gene Expression

● RNA polymerase (RNAP): the name of the enzyme used in transcription
● Messenger RNA (mRNA): the name given to the new strip that is made
● Maximum number of proteins made by one strip of mRNA: about 900

Epigenetics
Gene Genies ◉

* A genetic artist that sits on top of a genome
* Chemically modifies a genome's expression
* Epigenetic changes don't alter DNA

Epigenetics

A mysterious spirit beyond nature and nurture, I am a chemical overlay that determines the patterns of genes that are expressed. I can make any cell type in your body—muscle, nerve, skin—just by expressing or switching off and by boosting or muting Gene. I explain why one identical twin might have asthma when the other doesn't. Pure Gene-ius!

● Number of cell types in the human body: 210
● Genes inside tightly coiled DNA strands are off-limits (essentially "turned off")
● Epigenome: a set of chemical markers that control how the genome is expressed

Chapter 3
Biohacker Crew

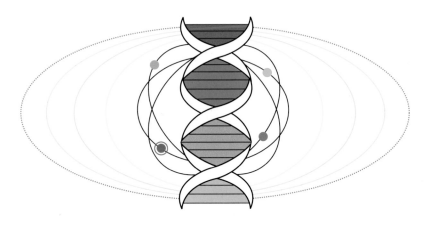

This totally twisted crew hangs out at the final frontier of science, probing the very limits of life itself. Hacking into the genomes of bacteria and adding in new parts and functions, these Biomasters reboot DNA, reprogram biological systems, and can even build Gene Genie Genome from scratch. Sharing a love of the thermal cycler, this bunch of gene weavers can cut, slice, and splice genes, remixing the genome to find out what each part does. These dudes and their systems will shortly create a fourth kingdom of life—the synthetic kingdom. Oh, and they'll all be wearing "designer genes!" *Boom bio-boom*!

Gene Splicing

GFP

Cre/loxP

Polymerase
Chain Reaction

Genetically
Modified
Organism

Cloned
Organisms

Synthetic
Biology

Synthetic Life

Shmeat

Biosafety

Gene Splicing
◉ Biohacker Crew

※ The key to making genetic modifications (GM stuff)
※ Cuts and pastes genes to make fresh living code
※ Creates new DNA called "recombinant DNA" (rDNA)

Snip! Snip! I'm a remix master. My speciality lies in stripping out tiny strands of DNA from one organism and knitting them into the DNA fabric of another.

Scientists use me when they want to take a desirable trait from one organism and put it into another. For example, some organisms produce proteins that protect them from insect attacks—an excellent trait for a plant. Scientists use my skills to isolate the gene containing the instructions for making these proteins, to chop out the sequence, and to slip it into a plant genome. My "scissors" are special proteins called restriction enzymes that cut and prize apart DNA's double strand. I load the genetic message into a loop of bacterial DNA, and this invades other cells, smuggling in my DNA delivery at the same time. It's the splice of life!

● First recombinant DNA: 1971 (Paul Berg)
● First biotech product: 1982 (Humulin—human insulin)
● First commercial GM crop: 1994 ("Flavr Savr" tomato)

Gene Splicing

GFP
◉ Biohacker Crew

✸ GFP is short for "green fluorescent protein"
✸ Isolated from jellyfish, this protein glows under ultraviolet light
✸ Used in biosensors and as a "reporter gene" (a genetic label)

A Day-Glo dream child, I'm a groover at the genetics disco. Bioscientists go crazy for my gene because they can use it to test their genetic tinkerings. They stick it on a piece of rDNA, just behind the gene that they want to test. If the new gene expresses (functions), it turns on my gene, which pumps out GFP, signaling a YES in wild colors. Oh yeah—I've got the moves.

GFP

● Number of amino acids in GFP: 238
● Living species from which GFP was first isolated: *Aequorea victoria* (a jellyfish)
● Discovered: 2008 (Martin Chalfie, Osamu Shimomura, Roger Y. Tsien)

Cre/loxP
Biohacker Crew ◉

* Highlights the jobs that genes do by switching them off
* Used to target genes in certain cells and tissue types in mice
* Can be activated when biochemical conditions change

Cre/loxP

Genetic trickery in one *knockout* package, I can get Gene to whisper its deepest secrets to me. But instead of allowing Gene to express itself (as you might expect), I "knock it out." You see, when Gene stops operating, a body can't do certain things or stop other things from happening, making it fairly easy to figure out which function Gene has.

● First "knockout mouse": 1989 (Mario R. Capecchi, Martin Evans, Oliver Smithies)
● Number of genes in a mouse: approx. 25,000
● Similarity of mouse genome to human genome: 70–90% (85% on average)

Polymerase Chain Reaction

◉ Biohacker Crew

☀ A mechanical process for reproducing genetic material
☀ The PCR machine is the workhorse of any genetics laboratory
☀ Used in forensic DNA fingerprinting and medical screening

Think of me as a huge copycat! Like a photocopier for genes, I churn out copies of short stretches of DNA—handy when there's only a tiny sample from, say, a crime scene.

I work best in a hot protein bath. At 200 °F (95 °C), the double helix of a piece of template DNA separates into two single-stranded chains. Cooling down to 130 °F (55 °C), "primer proteins" kick-start the transcription process by binding onto the ends of those strands. Then, at about 165 °F (74 °C), an enzyme called Taq polymerase rebuilds the double helix by pulling out nucleotide bases from the "bathwater" and sticking them onto the template strand. After about one hour (30 cycles), I've made a few micrograms' worth of DNA . . . Yowzers!

● PCR replication speed: about 1,000 bases per minute
● Human replication speed: about 2,000 bases per minute
● Rate of error: about 1 base in every 100,000

Polymerase
Chain Reaction

Genetically Modified Organism

◉ Biohacker Crew

✳ "Designer" organism whose genetic material is altered
✳ Created by scientists using gene-splicing techniques
✳ Current uses include research, agriculture, and drugs

Made to order and designed for life, I'm a supermodel. With the help of Gene Splicing and its rDNA, I can take the form of an organism that has never existed before.

Just imagine . . . lambs engineered to grow fat that is not as unhealthy to eat. Or microbugs whose genomes are altered to produce life-saving drugs. And what about food crops with a genetically engineered resistance to pests and diseases, so that farmers can produce bigger harvests? Or plants kitted out with genes from arctic fish that can survive frosts, thanks to the antifreeze protein in their leaves? Yes, I am all of these things and more. Forget GMO, surely it's more a case of OMG!

● First GM animal: 1974 (a mouse, engineered by Rudolf Jaenisch)
● Area of world's GM crops: 571,430 sq. mi. (1,480,000km^2)
● Area of GM crops in the U.S.A.: 257,916 sq. mi.(668,000km^2)

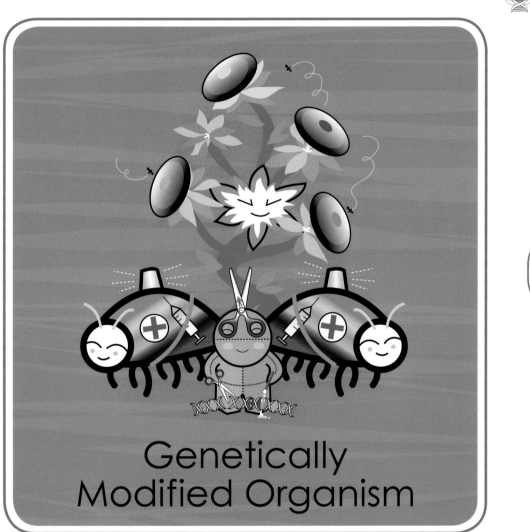

Genetically Modified Organism

Cloned Organisms
◉ Biohacker Crew

☀ Living things with the same genetic makeup as their parents
☀ Cloning occurs naturally in plants and some animals
☀ Produced to keep "pure" traits that might be lost in breeding

Welcome to the flock. We're a collective of 100-percent identical organisms. Created artificially, the genomes of our offspring are exactly the same as those of their parents. There's simply no telling us apart.

Living things that reproduce sexually—like you humans—mix their genes each time they do so. But grow a houseplant from a leaf cutting and you're cloning that plant. The breakthrough was taking this idea into the lab. Take an egg cell, suck out its nucleus, and inject into it the cell nucleus of the animal that you want to clone. Carefully monitored, this modified cell can be persuaded to divide and grow, just like a normal fertilized egg cell does. Implanted into a mother's womb, it is then born in the usual way. So far, this has worked with cows, pigs, monkeys, and sheep. *Baa!*

● First artificially cloned animal: born in 1996 (Dolly the Sheep, U.K.)
● Number of failed attempts before Dolly: 275
● Dolly's age at death: Six years

Cloned Organisms

Synthetic Biology
◉ Biohacker Crew

☀ Creator of specially designed organisms not found in nature
☀ Uses "BioBricks" to make man-made biosystems
☀ Offers tantalizing, yet scary, possibilities for the future

My game is to make artificial biological systems using a combo of biology and engineering. Unlike old-fashioned GMO, which mixes bits and pieces from animals and plants, I aim to modify microbes with completely new bits of DNA.

My standardized genetic parts connect like biological building blocks to make "gene machines." In the right hands, I'll create useful, living devices—a bacterial biodetector that senses water pollution and signals its find by expressing GFP, for example. No one wants these microbes to turn bad and overcome the natural defenses of Earth's living things, so I am designed in such a way that I can't reproduce. Don't fear, though, I lack the millennia of survival training that your genes have had and wouldn't last for two seconds outside of my fermenter.

● Number of registered Standard Biological Parts: more than 3,400
● First synthesized viral genome: 7742-base polio virus (created in 2002)
● First synthesized bacterial genome: 582,970 base-pair *Mycoplasma* (in 2008)

Synthetic Biology

Synthetic Life
◉ Biohacker Crew

☀ The first living thing whose parent is a computer!
☀ Designed in a "dry lab" rather than a "wet lab"
☀ "Synthia" was the first synthetic life form in the world

Neat, tidy, and well turned out, I am living, breathing biology designed by humans. One hundred percent manufactured, I'm a synthetic superstar—slimmer, fitter, and more productive than the real thing.

I create new genomes for cells—new DNA software systems. The cell is the hardware that reads the code and turns it into the chemicals that make life run smoothly. I operate in tried-and-tested ways, but I am utterly different to life as fashioned by natural selection. Boy, is evolution messy! It creates sprawling, untidy genomes, with all kinds of random "junk"—stuttering repeats of code and defunct genes. My newly minted genomes, by contrast, are designed by a computer to use the minimum number of genes necessary for life. Now that *is* neat!

● Creation of Synthia (*Mycoplasma mycoides* JCVI-syn1.0): in 2010 (Craig Venter)
● Cost of producing Synthia: more than $40 million
● Minimum set of genes that can sustain life: 382

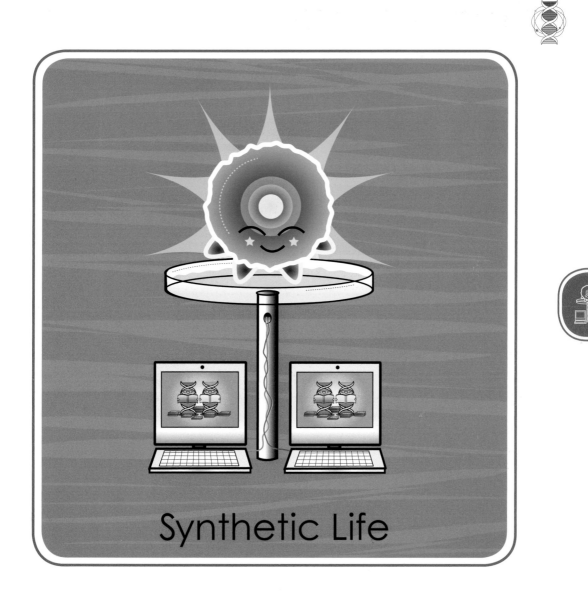

Synthetic Life

Shmeat
◉ Biohacker Crew

☀ Test-tube meat that is artificially grown from muscle cells
☀ Reared in the lab rather than out in the fields
☀ May some day make eating any other meat seem cruel

I am one cultured dude. Yeah! A peace-loving vegetarian, I'm the ethical choice for meat-eating humans. I bear no relation to imitation meat made from soy proteins. No way, man—I'm the real deal! Some day, you will buy a cell line at the supermarket, pop it into a tabletop bioreactor in your kitchen, and have a burger ready for dinner.

Shmeat

● Earliest demonstration of tissue culture: chicken, 1885 (Wilhelm Roux)
● First edible form: goldfish fillets (2000)—as a potential food for astronauts
● Price of beef Shmeat: about $1 million for 9 oz. (250g) (2009)

Biosafety

Biohacker Crew ◉

* ✳ This patrolman keeps a sharp eye on biohazards
* ✳ Ensures that no harmful bugs escape from the lab
* ✳ Also acts as a moral guardian for genetics

Biosafety

I make sure bioscience labs operate safely. My rules for working with biological agents range from level 1: noninfectious bugs—to level 4: deadly pathogens. They stop nasties escaping and dictate the measures that must be taken in the event of an accident. I also have my eye on practices that might accidentally (or otherwise) create a killer GM superbug.

* ● Bug examples: Level 1: chickenpox; Level 4: smallpox
* ● Level 1 containment: Hand washing and use of disinfectants in the lab
* ● Level 4 containment: High-level security, UV-light room, multiple air locks

Chapter 4
Medical Mavericks

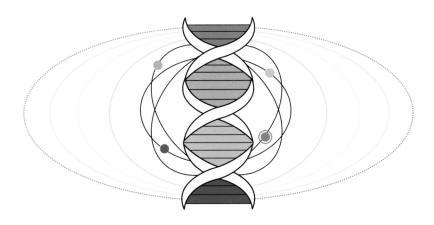

These bouncing bioscience buddies cover the techniques and technologies that are currently rocking the antiseptic-stinkin' corridors of the medical world. Plucky lifesavers, these guys will stop at nothing to help keep you alive and kicking. They get drugs to the sites that really need them—fast. They are more cunning than older treatments and use nanotechnology and bioengineering to target their treatments. When it comes to scalpel-and-forceps surgery, they are doing their best to reduce trauma to patients and managing to pull off some incredible stunts, such as transplanting entire faces.

Nanomedicine

Monoclonal Antibodies

Broad Spectrum Antivirals (BSAs)

Pharming

Biosensor

Face Transplant

Regenerative Medicine

Gene Therapy

Functional MRI

Nanomedicine
◉ Medical Mavericks

✳ Delivers health-giving treatment in miniscule measures
✳ Can offer more precise, less invasive medical procedures
✳ Mostly tested on mice so far

A pocket-size rocket, I'm a teeny-weeny type who packs a thunderbolt punch. I bring the wow-science of nanotechnology to the fusty old world of medicine.

I work on scales 1,000 times smaller than a human hair, which just happens to be the same size as many of your body's working parts (think cells and proteins). Injected into the body, I can travel in swarms and get to work right at the spot where repair is needed. There's nothing I can't do (in theory)! I can deliver drugs to specific tissues and, because of my size, I can slip inside a cell's membrane. My silky skills also help out with no-pain injections. If I wanted to, I could mend damaged hearts, seek and destroy cancer cells, and zap tumors. The trouble is, I'm still waiting on approval for use in human beings.

● 1 nanometer (nm) = 1 millionth of a millimeter (mm)
● Nanofiber diameter: less than 0.001mm
● Number of nanotech-based drugs currently being developed: more than 130

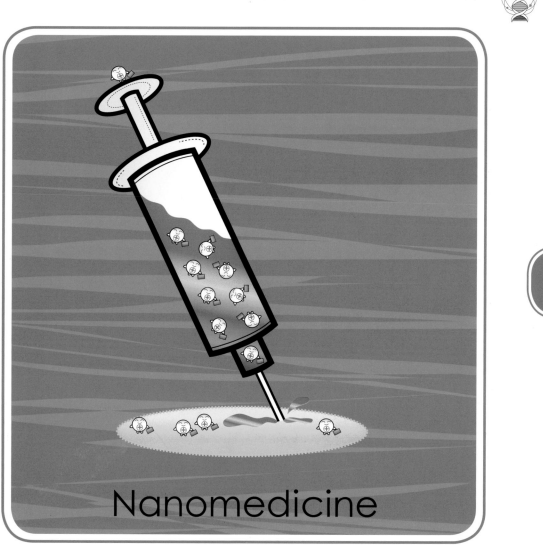

Nanomedicine

Monoclonal Antibodies

◎ Medical Mavericks

✳ Genetically engineered to target disease-causing organisms
✳ Made by cloned cells, so can be made in unlimited amounts

Identical "magic bullet" bounty hunters for your body, we cruise the highways on the lookout for intruders. When we find 'em, we waste 'em in a hail of protein-jacketed ammo. We're called out when a body's natural immune system rejects a transplanted organ following life-saving surgery. We also have top ranking in the fight against cancer.

Monoclonal Antibodies

● Discovery: 1975 (Georges Köhler, César Milstein, and Niels Kaj Jerne)
● Nobel Prize for discovery: 1984 (awarded to the above scientists)
● Early monoclonal antibody drug: Herceptin, 1998 (breast cancer treatment)

Broad Spectrum Antivirals (BSAs)

Medical Mavericks ◉

※ Target viruses in the way that antibiotics target bacteria
※ So far, scientists are unsure whether they also kill *good* viruses

Broad Spectrum Antivirals (BSAs)

Viral intruders, beware! HIV, rhinovirus, rabies, flu, dengue fever, Japanese encephalitis, hepatitis B, Ebola, herpes, norovirus—I'm after those dudes. And rather than target 'em one-by-one, I wanna kill 'em all in one go. My strategies include boosting natural defenses and interfering with virus DNA. They ain't got long to live, I can tell you!

● Number of offspring created by a cold virus within 24 hours: 16 million
● Most commonly used antiviral: Acyclovir (antiherpes drug)
● Number of viruses in saliva: 100 million viruses per milliliter

Pharming
◉ Medical Mavericks

✶ The use of genetic engineering to make medicinal proteins
✶ Involves splicing specific genes into plants and animals
✶ Produces drugs such as human insulin for diabetes sufferers

Chewing on a genetically modified strand of straw, I'm the pharmer of the phuture. My plants and animals are genetically modified so that their recombinant DNA produces pharmaceutical drugs. It may be phreaky, but it's phantastic phun, I can assure you. *Yee-haw!*

I get plants and animals to produce therapeutic drugs with a little help from Gene Splicing's cutting-edge biotechnology. Until recently, I used mainly microbes, such as the bacteria *E. coli* and yeast, to make my recombinant proteins in large bioreactors. These days, my "drug factories" might be goats, sheep, and cows, producing protein in their milk or blood. Taking your medicine now is as easy as drinking a glass of milk or crunching into a carrot. See you at the hoedown.

● First transgenic ewe (female sheep): 1990 (Tracy)
● First approved drug from goat's milk: 2009 (an anti-blood-clotting agent)
● First approved drug from transgenic carrot: 2009 (therapy for Gaucher's disease)

Pharming

Biosensor

◉ Medical Mavericks

✳ Bioengineered monitor used for detecting chemicals
✳ Many times more responsive than a human detector
✳ Uses include drug discovery and pollution monitoring

I'm a sensitive soul, used for detecting the presence of a certain chemical or reaction in a substance—I keep my beady eye on whatever you ask me to and sing like a canary if I spot even the slightest of changes!

I'm built using a biomaterial that is sensitive to the chemical ingredients under observation—enzymes, say, or antibodies, DNA or RNA, body tissues, or genetically engineered microorganisms. The biomaterial's reaction with the detected substance is converted into a signal, which is picked up and displayed on an output reader. Built into handy pens, I provide a way for diabetic sufferers to keep an eye on their blood-sugar levels. Ultramodern systems often use biohacked microbes, such as GFP, detectable using optical, electrical, or chemical sensors. Shine on!

● First biosensor: 1969 (Leland C. Clark)
● Things biosensors can detect: viruses, bacteria, hormones, drugs, pollutants
● "Critter on a chip": light-sensitive, bioluminescent-bacteria-coated computer chip

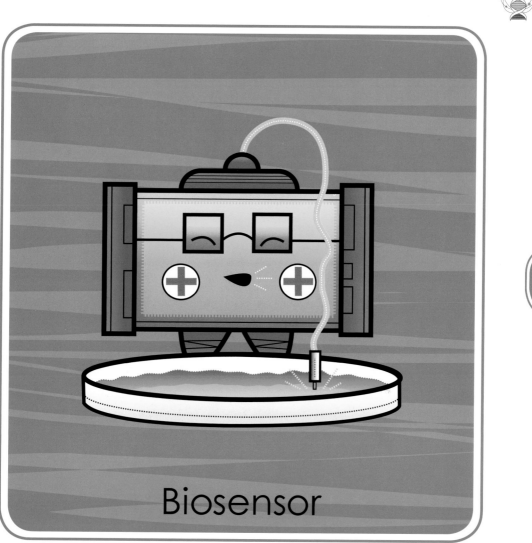

Biosensor

Face Transplant
◉ Medical Mavericks

※ Medical procedure that replaces a person's face
※ Face is matched in terms of size, color, and gender
※ Immune-system-suppressing drugs help prevent rejection

Don't confuse me with the ghoulish, Frankenstein-type experiments you might have read about. For people who have lost part or all of their face through disease, birth defects, or following horrible injuries—gunshot wounds or burns—I am a life changer. That's right, with me firmly attached, a dude can feel ready to *face* the world.

I involve a long and painstaking surgical operation. A damaged face is removed in its entirety—skin, blood vessels, fatty underlayer—and a new face is reconnected to the underlying blood vessels and nerves. Once the scars fade, the result is an interesting blend of donor and patient, with the flexible new face taking on the patient's original expressions. I have been known to bring back long-forgotten senses such as smell—that's nothing to sniff at!

● First living-human face transplant: 2005 (partial, France); 2010 (total, Spain)
● Duration of surgery: 8–15 hours
● Number of muscles required: to smile: 12; to frown: 11

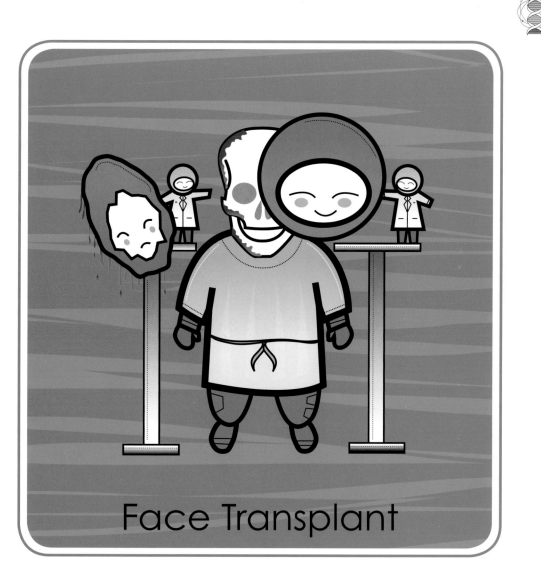

Face Transplant

Regenerative Medicine

◉ Medical Mavericks

✴ Body parts grown in a bioreactor and implanted surgically
✴ Grown from a patient's own tissue, so parts aren't rejected
✴ "Progenitor" cells can become any type of tissue in a body part

Forget transplant surgery or operations to replace worn-out body parts with artificial joints—that's nothing. I can access the genetic information that's in every cell of your body to magic up brand-new body parts. Now that's *pixie dust!*

Each type of body cell has the potential to regrow itself—it's just a question of making it happen. I take a biomaterial frame printed on a 3-D printer, coat it with special cells, and bathe it in growth factor. I can rustle up blood vessels on a doughnut scaffold of nanofibers, while a spray of my progenitor cells causes skin to regrow over burns—without scarring. I can do bladders, bones, ears, fat, intestines, veins, skin, and soon I'll manage eyes and kidneys. I kid you not!

● Maximum regrowth of tissue: 0.4 in. (1cm)
● Natural tissue regenerators: salamanders (limbs, tail, and even an eye)
● "Earmouse" created: 1995 (Dr. Charles Vacanti and Dr. Linda Griffith-Cima)

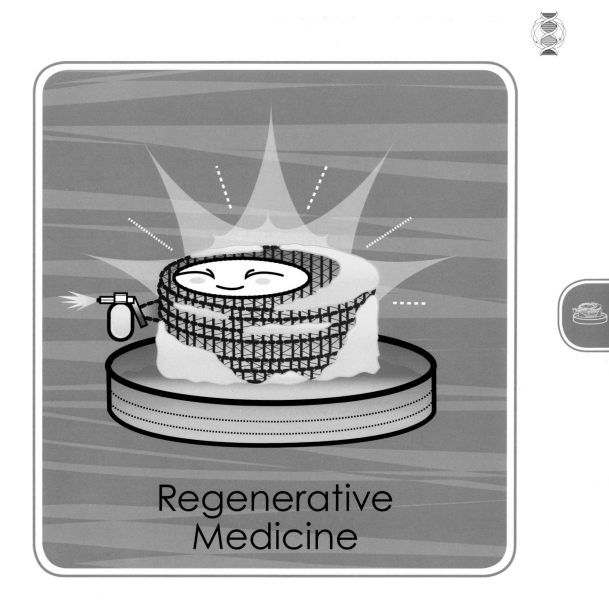

Regenerative
Medicine

Gene Therapy

◉ Medical Mavericks

☀ Using DNA to help treat genetic disorders
☀ Involves replacing mutated genes with new DNA
☀ A relatively new technique, yet to be fully explored

Not all diseases come from external bugs invading the body—some come from within the genome. Alterations of the DNA code—called mutations—can prevent a gene from doing its job correctly, resulting in inheritable disorders that can plague families for generations.

Enter little old me! Sneaking into the body on board a virus or via a direct injection, I swap in for the disease-causing gene. I can also knock out a misfiring gene or introduce an entirely new gene to help fight a disease. Once inside the cell, the new DNA (that's me) starts to express its therapeutic, health-giving proteins, and the symptoms of the sufferer are eased. More of a hope than a reality at the moment, but I'm bound to catch on once geneticists work out exactly where these mutations lie.

● Inventors of gene therapy: Friedmann and Roblin (1972)
● Genetic disorders include: cystic fibrosis, hemophilia, and Huntington's disease
● Types of viruses used: adeno-associated virus (AAV), lentivirus, herpes simplex virus

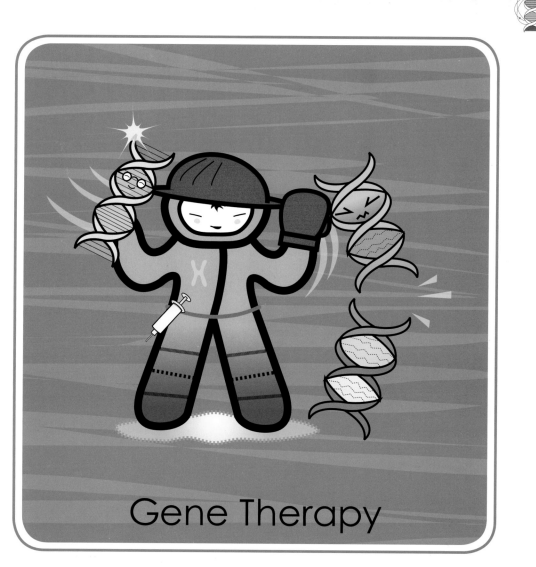

Gene Therapy

Functional MRI

◉ Medical Mavericks

✳ Superstrength magnetic field used for imaging the body
✳ Works by detecting and monitoring blood flow
✳ Vaccine-, surgery-, and radiation-free

A superhero with the power to see right through you, there's nothing old-fashioned about me. No run-of-the-mill x-ray vision here—no, sir! Eat your heart out, Superman.

I am just one technique applied using an MRI scanner. My very strong magnetic field surrounds a narrow central tube in a machine big enough to swallow humans. I can spot tumors and soft-tissue damage that's too small to see using x-rays. I can also watch the bleeps and flickers of your brain ticking over. My images show how oxygen carried in the blood ebbs and flows in response to particular parts of the brain working out. I've discovered some pretty crazy stuff—for example, the brain lights up a full seven seconds before a choice is made, showing that decisions are made before we are even conscious of them. *Spooky!*

● Brain-scanning rate: every 2–3 seconds
● Typical MRI field strengths: 1.5 and 3 tesla
● Magnetic field strength of Earth: 25,000–65,000 nT (nanotesla)

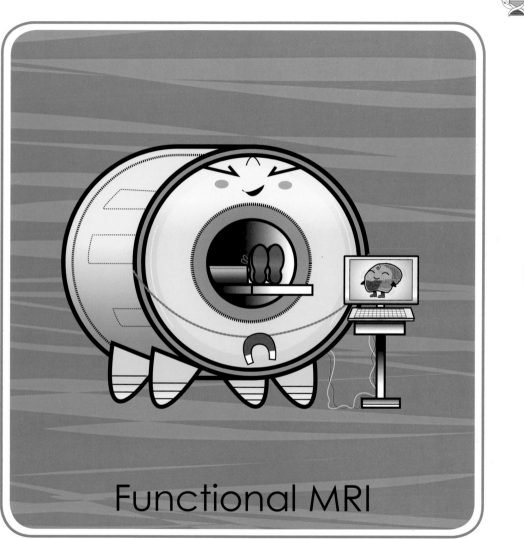

Functional MRI

Glossary

Bacterium A single-celled organism; most living things on this planet are bacteria of one type or another. Genetics bioscience often involves bacteria, because they are relatively simple and easy to grow in the lab.

Biodetector Part of a biosensing system; can discover the presence of a particular substance, such as a toxin, bacterium, or virus, or "notice" a change in a certain property, such as electricity, pressure, or pH.

Biofuel A fuel (solid, liquid, or gas) that is made by organisms or is refined from the body parts or waste material of living things.

Biomaterial The stuff of living things, from their bodies to their cellular building blocks, DNA, and genes, including substances manufactured by organisms.

Bioreactor A containing device that houses a colony of living things and keeps them alive while they undergo a chemical or biological process; often used for growing tissue cells or cultures (*see also*: Fermenter; Thermal cycler).

Biosystem The interacting internal parts of an organism or an interconnected system of living things.

Biotech Any technology that manipulates life forms to provide something useful. Beekeeping and beer making are ancient forms of biotech; modern biotech makes use of recombinant DNA (rDNA).

Catalyze To increase the rate of a chemical process or decrease the energy needed to start a reaction; in humans, enzymes act as catalysts.

Cell The basic building block of all living things; a tiny, organic structure containing chemicals and biochemical "machinery." In the center of a cell is the nucleus, which stores the organism's genome.

Dry lab A slang biotech term for labs that only have computers in them and no "sloppy" genetic experiments involving real living things.

Enzyme A biological catalyst that enables many functions in the body. Almost all biochemical reactions require enzymes, which are crucial to DNA replication. Enzymes are proteins.

Fermenter A type of bioreactor in which a colony of bacteria, such as yeast, is fed nutrients that the bacteria turn into sugars; fitted with a heat exchanger or refrigerated to keep the interior at a constant temperature. "Fermenter" can also be used casually to refer to any kind of bioreactor.

Invertebrate An animal that does not have a backbone; spineless animals include worms, bugs, beetles, and insects, as well as many sea creatures.

Metabolism Body processes that take place inside the cell; all the biochemical reactions that keep an organism alive.

Microbe A microorganism: a bug or a germ; a bacterium or a virus.

Natural selection The process that drives evolution: only those individuals that are well adapted to their environment survive to reproduce and pass on their genes.

Nucleotide The basic structural unit of DNA.

Nucleus The small, central core of a cell that holds the complete DNA "library" (the genome) of an organism.

Organism A fancy term for a living thing; a single life form.

Progenitor cell Internal organs (body parts) are made of many different types of specialized cells, such as muscle, lining or connective tissue, as well as cells that do special jobs. While many organs produce stem cells that can only become one type of cell, progenitor cells are a type of stem cell that have the potential to become several types of specialized cells. They are often used by the body to repair damage.

Radiation The emission of energetic particles from radioactive materials, which can do harm to cells and DNA.

Replicate The process of copying DNA.

Tardigrade A small, water-dwelling animal with eight legs, also known as a water bear or moss piglet.

Telomeres Repeating pieces of DNA on the ends of chromosomes. They protect the "active" part of a chromosome from damage during replication.

Thermal cycler Also known as a PCR machine, the thermal cycler is an amplifier for DNA. Used in every genetics lab, it uses the polymerase chain reaction (PCR) to reproduce many copies of the same DNA sequence.

Trait A characteristic, such as eye color or susceptibility toward diabetes, that is inherited and expressed through the genes.

Transgenic A genetically engineered organism that has some of its genes taken from another, unrelated living thing.

Virus A tiny, infectious agent that is about 100 times smaller than a bacterium. Viruses cannot reproduce themselves—instead, they reproduce by hijacking the replication systems of other cells. Viruses can infect any life form.

Wet lab A slang biotech term for a genetics lab where experiments with living organisms are carried out.

Index